TO BE READ IN THE DARK

TO BE READ IN THE DARK

POEMS BY
MAXINE CHERNOFF

OMNIDAWN PUBLISHING
RICHMOND, CALIFORNIA
2011

Cover photo; *Icicles in Window* courtesy of Corbis Images

Cover and Interior Design by Cassandra Smith

Typefaces: Adobe Garamond Pro and Trajan Pro

Printed on Finch 60# Recycled 30% PCW Natural Opaque Vellum

Library of Congress Cataloging-in-Publication Data

Chernoff, Maxine, 1952-
To be read in the dark : poems / by Maxine Chernoff.
p. cm.
ISBN 978-1-890650-61-2 (pbk. : alk. paper)
I. Title.
PS3553.H356T6 2011
811'.54--dc23
2011029082

Published by Omnidawn Publishing, Richmond, California
www.omnidawn.com   (510) 237-5472   (800) 792-4957
10 9 8 7 6 5 4 3 2 1
ISBN: 978-1-890650-61-2

Poems have appeared in Denver Quarterly, the Omnidawn Blog, and The Nation

for you

THE BOX

you and I

and the world

in the box

the world

blue as memory's

alien air

you

blue as

the world

dust motes

gleaming

in the corners

historically rich

in potential

the box is not

the room's

white curtains

or the camera's

closed eye

the construction

of a sentence

enters the box

leaves the world

unsaid

There Will Be Consequences

memory's edge

is too demanding

asks for reaching

when it only

wants models

show me a list

memory says

you reveal

cardboard scenery

a sheriff's badge

and slippery stones

anything please

for memory's sake

a few spare pigeons

a haunted zoo

your field of vision

seems to be failing

you prop it up

with ambition

in its circumference

there are blackbirds

your childhood

wants to have

a party

your attendance

is required

you'll conjure up

some glass begonias

cameras please

memory says

ENDINGS

you take the thread

dear taster of endings

warp or woof

an amorous quest

involving the greening

of translated ground

you take the words

like any blamed object

make them excessive

like crow's mimicry

you breathe in their weather

exhale a death

night's airy gestures

are over-determined

valor is pale

you ask for a window

to open a reason

for feeding on light

like any dead thing

you want some comfort

in room's sentenced story

verbless black corner

changing your essence

like cave's allegory

Marginalia

The essence

of essence

is essence and razors

the essence

of certainty

razors and truth

the plow turns around

and that is a verse

intangible subject

grounded in syntax

I hereby give notice

to all my familiars

that fusion in nature

results in a crime

he wrote the epic

for the army of ants

whose lost civilization

was bottle-cap size

he wrapped it in pine needles

ineffable treatise

of sticks and dust

a cannibal's art

is pastiche at best

the last great theory

presented a risk

we had to seclude it

for its own good

the clock met its maker

the shirt its iron

steam filled the air

and afternoon chill

How I Wrote Certain of my Books

The mountain's white page

got lost in the story

as did the knowledge

of caves' deep plunge

a woman sat weeping

for the sake of description

and sailors embarked

from paper's smooth shore

like invisible birds

caught up in the mind

God exists

but not the world

involving the difference

of moonlight and harbor

the second of telling

becomes the told

a cold white cheek

stood in a doorframe

he called it a name

and it turned his way

this often happens

among the living

who articulate intention

by rumor and theory

invisible ledger

of garden's dark soil

written by snails

with faulty logic

unless our garments

get shredded by truth

we keep what we lose

despite light's inclination

THE NEWS

The inhuman among us
want to sing as others
they have a sacred place
constructed of their crimes
that surely corresponds
to something in the world
their subtle lack of grace
makes it strange and rich
singing accusations
in a pure contralto
which almost sounds
like truth dressed up
as a prince
or darkness curling under
an open well-lit door

To Harbor

longing makes

its own perfection

maps the clouds'

unerring substance

smoothes the edge

of variation

a woman

harbors affection

for a castle

she once saw

on dream's mapped page

restriction's grace

is automatic

death to words

in moonlit beds

Dickinson's Waifs on Niedecker's Shore

All that sunlight

lost in the hollows

of an eye

the catastrophe

accomplished

smoothly

like dictation

no one comes

to say farewell

or even good-bye

you spilling

like an overfilled

cup   like a lake

in April

you cold and shivering

then a brief flash

of embroidery

mushrooms or birds

or your name

in black thread

AVIARY

pity birds' winter

icy torpor

of nature reduced

to want and shadow

an alibi is

a frozen witness

to end where it ends

is only digression

a story is whole

without a staircase

moon's dictation

unread in the dark

to pantomime loss

is tragedy's license

finitude, please,

frozen ground says

A Bed on Fire

the smiling assassin

isn't a dream

what is embodied

asks us to listen

beyond rooms

the doctor has scissors

the hour, confessions

a lingering fable

serves up

its ghosts

intention burns

like any ember

GOD'S EVENING

he is tired

of pity's mansion

tired of Sunday

and its cautions

even with loss

he is complacent

from where he sits

he sees a landscape

several lemons

and a book

media studies

is his interest

one of several

he will tell you

no longer eager

for approval

his children's sorrow

is a bad novel

touching his hair

he reads a survey

he'll sleep all night

emptied of pronouns

LANDSCAPE

an island concealed

by spring excess

is only water and idea

a certain moth

with lattice wings

is a coda

for the season

fear the argument

fear its maker

a milliner

with certain pretensions

for him

everything

is hats

no trunks no leaves

no necessary

or unnecessary

prisms

shame is anything

but dark

ELEGY

the naked truth is leaning

like any propped-up door

catastrophe's perspective

slips into the scene

when the author with his cape

untells the story's end

suppose it tears in half

like any fought-over letter

or botches its one chance

sweet caged bird

under the harsh light

of meaning's condescension

death is not the star

it is only scene

the book is closed again

The Language

a field

of black sheep

who know

Church Latin

a shipyard

of vessels

all named Sentence

a tangle of words

in a basket

of laundry

a night

like no other

blackbirds falling

like endings

a gift

unrecognized

by grace

a barrel

only a barrel

at the Stoics' Hotel

they stay for years

getting lost

in the language

DECEMBER 31

any sparrow

on a branch

defines a doctrine

of catalogue or hymn

in-between

-ness a genre

left to private song

a species attends

to its music

what is isolate

remains attached

to silence

let this stick be X

this witness Y

voiceless coda

to the day

Threshold

God on the tarmac

wants to know

how systems work

he wants the rules

in clear block letters

which in principal

he can read

in any language

but right now

he wants only Spanish

which he remembers

from when he was young

just in knickers

slicked-back hair

when shiny mirrors

mirrored him

oh wait he remembers

a play he once saw

moving as well as

supremely clear

God is nostalgic

for simple instructions

on how to open

or close a box

he never knows when intervention

will breed ineptitude or shame

his shame alone is nameless he thinks

and then he peels and eats an orange

there must be a word

for its bitter rind

What Did You Do in the War?

memory's acres

stained with knowing

white uniforms

deciphered

in a flashlight's

half-ironic curl

the eastern edge

of slippage

results in

more story

as dissolving

makes clear

its capacity

for interpretation

syllables stretching

beyond recognition

moments reduced

to cicada and vision

Maxine Chernoff published her first two books of poems in 1976. Since then she has published 12 books of poetry including *World* and *Evolution of the Bridge* (Salt Publications) and *Among the Names* and *The Turning* (Apogee Press) and *Without*, to appear from Shearsman in spring of 2012. In addition, she is the author of six books of fiction including the *New York Times* Notable Book of stories, *Signs of Devotion* (Simon and Schuster, 1994). In 2009, she won the PEN USA Translation Award for *Selected Poems of Friedrich Hölderlin* (Omnidawn), co-translated with Paul Hoover. She co-edits the long-running journal *New American Writing* and has chaired the Creative Writing Department at San Francisco State University since 1996.